Made in the USA
Las Vegas, NV
25 October 2024

10462243R00057